Miles Christmas Surprise

Written By
Carmen Andersen

Copyright © 2018 by CSB Innovations • All rights reserved

Just North of the Snowy Mountain, and then left at the giant Iceberg sits a little town called Wintersburg.

It is in this town, where a young boy named Miles's life is turned upside down.

This year, he feared that there would be no presents under the tree, and no yummy ham to eat.

So Miles prayed for a way to save Christmas Day, and just when he began to doubt, he quickly learned what Christmas was truly all about.

Our plans are not always the plans of our Heavenly Father, but I bear my testimony to you.

That our Heavenly Father knows ALL the desires of our hearts, even the ones that can be found at the Frosties Toy Mart.

Things may not come right away, but have faith because things always have a way of working themselves out.

Miles loves to share and help those he lives near, so it makes sense that Christmas is his favorite time of the year.

In fact, the folk in Wintersburg knows that if you need help with anything from carrying groceries or shoveling snow, Miles is the boy to know!

At Ice Berg Elementary, where all the cool kids go at a table in the last row, sits Miles and his best friend Pete sharing something good to eat.

One day after treading home in the snow, Miles is surprised to see that his dad was already home.

His parents share the saddest of news, the plant that makes the Candy Cane Shoes has given his dad some really bad news.

With the factory not running, his dad's checks will no longer be coming.

Miles is feeling very blue and can't think of what to do; his biggest fear is having no Christmas to look forward to.

After he prays, he thinks of all the money he has earned throughout the year, and now he has a plan to save Christmas Day and spread Christmas Cheer.

He heads out the door to accomplish this, but first his chores he won't miss.

So he heads to the Murrays and shovels their snow in a hurry while he shares with them all of his worries. After hearing of Miles' distress, Mr. and Mrs. Murray want to give him a check, but Miles refuses to accept.

He tells Mr. and Mrs. Murray that he will be okay, he has a plan to save Christmas day.

So he must get to Frosties as fast as he can to buy gifts for his family, and maybe even a ham.

Miles runs to Frosties and searches the store, but he cannot find what he is looking for.

As he is leaving the store, he sees a man standing by the front door, asking for money for the poor.

Without even a thought, Miles takes out some of the money he brought. He gives it to the man and then shakes his hand. Now, off to buy the family a ham, the biggest that will fit in mom's pan.

But while leaving the store, Miles sees something he cannot understand; a woman leaving with no groceries in her hands.

Something deep inside tells him to be kind, and so he has made up his mind!

Miles gives her the great big ham and simply says Merry Christmas ma'am.

On the long walk home, Miles passes his church and is quickly reminded that he is always being guided.

As the train station nears, guess who appears, none but an old man with a VERY long beard.

Much to Miles' despair, the man has no train fare. You see, he hasn't seen his family in over a year and wants to bask with them in their holiday cheer.

Miles holds his last five dollars in his hand and then hands it over to the old man. To show appreciations, the man tries to give Miles the only thing he has; an old family star. Miles says, "no, thanks," and watches while he boards the train car.

And so came another Christmas that started with snow, but a Christmas like this Miles had not yet known.

No presents to open or ham to be cooked, but somehow he knew he could be happy no matter how things looked.

Miles went downstairs and was ready for whatever the day might bring when suddenly the doorbell rang. Standing outside in spite of the flurry was Mr. and Mrs. Murray, who brought all of the gifts that were on Miles' shopping list.

With thank you hugs, the Murrays departed, and just when the unwrapping started, the doorbell rang again and there stood Pete, Miles' best friend.

Miles jaw dropped, and his eyes opened wide when he saw the woman he gave the ham to standing by Pete's side.

Just when Miles thought that the door could ring no more, it did indeed, but this time, he found no one at the door.

He only saw a beautifully wrapped box with a tag that said 'to Miles' on top. When Miles opened the box, he was surprised to find a beautiful star inside.

Inside further, Miles read a message that he will never forget "Every good deed should be followed by another" Signed Mr. Bingles.

That evening as Miles kneeled and said his prayers, his heart was truly thankful for what turned out to be the best Christmas yet.

The presents from the Murrays he did not expect, and who knew that he gave the ham to Pete's mom whom he had never met.

Last but not least, he was happy to learn that he had met Mr. Bingles, the richest man in Wintersburg's, according to the local gazette.

Heavenly Father had made all of Miles' Christmas dreams come true, just not the way Miles had planned.

Now, as I said concerning faith—that it was not a perfect knowledge—even so it is with my words. Ye cannot know of their surety at first, unto perfection, any more than faith is a perfect knowledge.

Ryan Juarez

Ryen Juarez is a 10-year-old aspiring singer, dancer, and actor. He loves to perform and considers the world his stage. Ryen is extremely friendly and outgoing, and is full of personality. He is a fan of Motown and musicals. Ryen's biggest fans are his close-knit family of six.

Colby W. Ulrich

Colby W. Ulrich is 10 years old and enjoys playing football with his dad. He is a Sweet kid and loves new adventures.

Barrett W. Swaim

Barrett W. Swaim wants to be an Engineer like his Dad. His passion is acting. He loves his family and loves to travel. He really loves New York.

Reese Bourne

Reese Bourne is 11 years old and wants to be a school teacher when she grows up. Reese loves to dance, ride horses, sing, and play basketball. Reese is very creative and smart.

Jeremiah Johnson

Jeremiah J. Johnson is 7 years old and wants to be in the NFL when he grows up. He loves to play football, run track, and play basketball. Jeremiah is sweet, caring and loves God.

Ellie Hunt

Ellie Hunt is 11 years old and wants to be an artist when she grows up. She spends her free time drawing, reading, and crafting. Ellie is a wonderful big sister and can't wait to be a babysitter.

Andrew Nicholson

Andrew Nicholson is 10 years old and wants to be a TV and Movie actor when he grows up. He likes to play basketball, ride bikes with his friends, listen to music, go to theatre camp, and watch movies. Andrew is a great big brother to his siblings Ian and Lucy.

www.csbinnovations.com

www.ingramcontent.com/pod-product-compliance
Lightning Source LLC
Chambersburg PA
CBHW041436010526
44118CB00002B/91